The Official Fonzie™ Scrapbook

by Ben Davidson

Publishers · GROSSET & DUNLAP · New York
A FILMWAYS COMPANY

Also by Ben Davidson:

The Skateboard Book

1978 PRINTING

Copyright © 1976 by Paramount Pictures Corporation
All rights reserved
Published simultaneously in Canada

Library of Congress catalog card number: 76-43195
ISBN 0-448-12885-3   (hardcover edition)
ISBN 0-448-12857-8   (paperback edition)

Printed in the United States of America

Fonzie, The Fonz, and "Happy Days" are registered
trademarks of Paramount Pictures Corporation

Acknowledgments

My sincere thanks to the following people who proved invaluable in putting this book together: Garry Marshall, Jerry Paris, and Bob Brunner, who took time out from their "Happy Days" madness to assist me; Earl Wingard and Pat Myers, from Paramount's publicity department; Anne, Melle, and Randi, my tireless editing and typing pool; and Phill, who calmly (I think) put up with the pre-publication mess that's cluttered our apartment for the past two months.

Contents

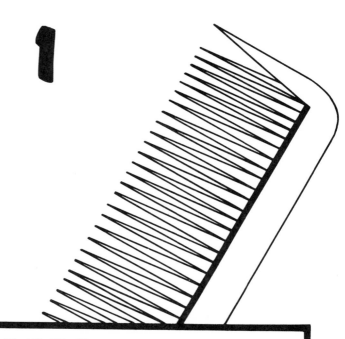

Enter
Arthur Fonzarelli

Enter Arthur Fonzarelli

By way of introduction . . . enter Arthur Fonzarelli, also known as Fonzie , also known as The Fonz . Bedecked in leather jacket, blue jeans, white T-shirt, and engineer boots, he is the epitome of toughness—a young man to whom the world is an arena in which one is forced to test one's power constantly if one is to survive. And the Fonz does this expertly, sometimes subtly, sometimes forcibly — but always with conviction.

As he dismounts from his bike (the bike

Ralph Malph picked up to replace the one he—Ralph—ran over with his car and demolished) and parks it in the Cunninghams' driveway, a shiny 1952 DeSoto cruises down the street. Fonzie looks at it and shakes his head with disgust—a DeSoto—how uncool can you get? He won't even get under the hood of a DeSoto to repair it except under the most extreme of circumstances. Professional ethics. It would be like a heavyweight boxer picking a fight with a baby.

And a professional he is. As a mechanic, as in many other realms, he has no peer. Once Fonzie's cousin, Spike (a miniature Fonzie), attempted to compliment him on being a "good" mechanic. "Not good," corrected Fonzie, "the best." If anyone can fix it, Fonzie can. And probably if *nobody* else can fix it, Fonzie can.

No one knows this better than Berkeley "Bronko" Van Alden. All had been well in Fonzie's professional life until his longtime employer, Herb, decided to sell the

Fonzie truly is the "Dear Abby of Arnold's." Amazing how such a hardnosed guy can be so sensitive to the plight of his friends and so willing to help when he can.

Back in his apartment, the first thing Fonzie does, even before he takes off his jacket, is go to the mirror. When he first moved into the Cunninghams', his only

In his bathroom "office" with Ralph, Fonzie truly is the "Dear Abby" of Arnold's.

Fonzie's basic kindness is shown again as he takes Laverne and Shirley's pigeons to the Cunningham's to care for them. © by Paramount Pictures Corporation

. . . But his act is foiled as the roof literally caves in.
© by Paramount Pictures Corporation

complaint revolved around mirrors—not enough of them. As he looks at his reflection (one of the joys of life), out of the corner of his eye he catches sight of the pictures of his girls on the opposite wall. They're arranged in a diamond configuration, those at the top being the girls who have . . . proved more valuable.

Girls are another aspect of Fonzie's life that hasn't changed much since his gang days. With a two-volume "little black book" covering some 2,000 chicks, it's an understatement to say that Fonzie has a way with women. Basically, his success can be attributed to his belief that "chicks like guys who are sophisticated, debonair, and cool—like Cary Grant, Clark Gable, and The Fonz." Good looks also help.

Fonzie's earliest recollection of his life with girls goes all the way back to kindergarten where he used to bury himself in the sandbox with chicks. More recent

proof of females' attraction to him came when he raised a tidy sum of money (so Richie and Potsie could take a little vacation) by selling kisses.

"When it comes to chicks," he once said, "The Fonz has a responsibility. I gotta be on call twenty-four hours a day." But it's

"Chicks like guys that are sophisticated, debonair, and cool . . ." © by Paramount Pictures Corporation

not advisable for any one girl to expect anything near that much attention. Explaining a problem he was having with a chick, Fonzie told the guys, "She was demanding too much of me. It got to where every time we went out, she wanted me to stay with her the whole time."

On Howard's forty-fifth birthday, Fonzie had to call the airport to cancel a reservation Mr. C. had booked on a flight to Hawaii. After he had been talking to the girl at the reservation desk for a while (about a few things other than airplane reservations) she asked him, "Hey, what makes you think you're so cool?" The Fonz hung up on her and a second later she called back. He picked up the phone and, before she could utter a word, said, "That's what makes me think I'm so cool." The Fonz has a power over women—case closed.

Of all Fonzie's worldly possessions, perhaps the most cherished is his motorcycle. Everybody around knew that, but it wasn't until the Cunninghams found Fonzie's bike strewn about in front of their house in pieces that anyone realized just how much he loved that machine. Fonzie was bereaved but Howard just couldn't understand his grief. "After all," he said, "it was just a motorcycle."

"Just a motorcycle," Fonzie replied in disgust. "And I suppose your mother was just a mother. This wasn't just a bike, it was a close friend."

But overlooking all the other amazing things about Fonzie, perhaps his most impressive trait is his self-respect. Having lived all those years on his own, The Fonz came to learn what he could and could not do (although there's actually not much in the latter category).

He has survived remarkably and gone beyond that—hence his confidence and self-esteem. Often that self-esteem borders on conceit. Once, when his plan to

"This bike made me what I am today."
© by Paramount Pictures Corporation

keep Ralph out of the Marines failed, he found it extremely difficult to admit that he was wrong. After being prodded and prodded to own up to his mistake, he finally tried. "I was wrr,wrr . . . It just gets stuck in my throat." Obviously the Fonz is not one to be humble. But in the main, his pride is based on fact. And when all is said and done, it has served him, and others, well.

"Maybe I wouldn't win any medals for good behavior," he told Spike, "But I never did anything I was ashamed of."

Fonzie opens a cupboard to look for something to eat. "I got beans, I got beans,

and I got beans," he thinks to himself. The Fonz is not much of a cook. Once he tried to cook a can of spaghetti by putting the whole thing, can and all, into a pot of boiling water. He doesn't even think it's his place to cook. "Ironing's okay," he once remarked. "But cooking—that's woman's work."

Well, nothing to eat. Fonzie flips on the radio. Elvis. That's cool. He flops down on his bed with the current issue of *Hot Rod* magazine. Suddenly there's a knock on the door. Fonzie puts the mag down and shakes his head as if to say, "I should've known I couldn't have a moment's peace."

"The Fonz is free," he yells.

The door opens and Richie walks in.

"Fonzie, I got a problem."

So what else is new?

Ralph turns over his worldly possessions to Fonzie as he prepares to join the Marines.
© by Paramount Pictures Corporation

Although he tries valiantly, Fonzie can't talk Ralph out of the Marines. In the end, Fonzie was "Wrrr . . . wrong." © by Paramount Pictures Corporation

2

In the Beginning— and into the Future

In the Beginning—
and into the Future

The year is 1970. The United States is preoccupied with the war in Vietnam and inflation. Student unrest lingers. The vitality of the Sixties is on the wane, leaving the country in a vague state of political, economic, and cultural tension. The Beatles have broken up. A good many people are asking themselves, "What now?"

What effects were these circumstances having in the entertainment world? One response involved shifting the thrust of literary, musical, and filmic emphasis to times that seemed more peaceful—or at least more understandable. Fifties nostalgia was becoming a big part of this apparent trend toward "past-oriented" entertainment. Some segments of the American population seemed to find the innocence of the Fifties comforting. No doubt there was safety to be found in times past. At the core of it (though we as a people seem to despise the word) was escapism—flight into memories, into a world that seemed harmless simply because it no longer existed.

In 1970, ABC-TV sought to go a step beyond Fifties nostalgia by doing a new version of a once highly popular television show set in the 1930s called "I Remember Mama." The logic seems apparent. If audiences find comfort in the Fifties, going back twenty years further would appear to be even more comforting.

Perhaps the quest for the unique was the intent. Although entertainment seems to rush in on us in strings of conformity, a singular, never-before-done (or at least not-recently-done) idea must precede the line of spin-offs, take-offs, and rip-offs.

The security-in-conformity factor aside, show business is always keeping an eye out for a new gimmick.

Out of the roster of ten or so comedy creators with reliable track records, and the twenty or so with semi-records, ABC-TV chose to approach Garry Marshall with the "I Remember Mama" concept. The choice was a good one. Along with Jerry Belson, Marshall had developed the hit TV series "The Odd Couple" and had written more than 100 situation-comedy episodes for such series as "The Danny Thomas Show," "The Lucy Show," and the original "Dick Van Dyke Show."

Garry Marshall, creator of "Happy Days."
© by Paramount Pictures Corporation

The Cunninghams—a nice warm family.
© by Paramount Pictures Corporation

The team has also written segments for "I Spy" and the "Bob Hope Chrysler Theatre" drama series and had created the NBC comedy series "Hey, Landlord." Their motion picture accomplishments were also impressive, for they had written and produced *How Sweet It Is* starring Debbie Reynolds and James Garner, and *The Grasshopper,* the critically acclaimed film starring Jacqueline Bisset.

So the offer was made, but Marshall turned it down. "I wasn't alive then. I had no interest in what was going on in the Thirties and I told the network I didn't want to do it," he recalls.

The basic concept of dealing with the past comedically did appeal to him, however, and he told ABC that although "I Remember Mama" wasn't exactly up his alley, he'd be interested in doing something with the Fifties. That was his "era," the period of his adolescence. It was a time that had sentimental appeal for him, one

with which he was familiar and in which he had interest.

So Marshall went to the drawing board and invented the Cunninghams, the typical and lovable family around which "Happy Days" now revolves (with the exception of an older son). The seed germinated and gave birth to a half-hour pilot called "A New Family in Town," starring Ron Howard, Anson Williams, and Marion Ross. All the characters were the same in the pilot as in the current series, except Fonzie, whose personality as we know it wasn't consistent with what Marshall describes as "a nice, warm family comedy."

This time, though, Marshall was on the disappointed end. ABC-TV simply wasn't interested. The pilot was eventually used as an episode in the series "Love American Style" and then shelved.

But as time passed, Fifties nostalgia began making headway. The Broadway musical "Grease," set in the Fifties, opened and became an immediate smash. The film *American Graffiti* was released and met with rave reviews and enthusiastic audiences. Coincidentally, Ron Howard co-starred in *Graffiti,* adding to what would become the misconception that "Happy Days" was a take-off on that motion picture. Unquestionably, the series did ride to success on the wake of *Graffiti,* but, for the record, the film was preceded by the original "Happy Days" pilot.

Suddenly, the success of these two productions (not to mention the rise of the Fifties rock-n-roll revival band Sha Na Na) shed new light on the "Happy Days" idea. The mass marketability of Fifties nostalgia became obvious to ABC-TV and the network contacted Marshall. According to Marshall, ABC-TV, in the person of Michael Eisner, was enthusiastic about developing "Happy Days," but with certain additions and revisions. Primarily, they felt the original pilot was "a little too soft and

16

warm" and not quite as funny as they thought it could be.

With *American Graffiti* as a point of reference, the network also saw the necessity of having a gang as one of the elements in a show that essentially revolved around a middle-class family. No doubt this aspect of the Fifties was an integral part of the period, but Marshall had reservations.

"I mumbled a little when they proposed it and went home and decided a gang wouldn't work. I felt Eisner was right in a sense; the show did need some other elements. So rather than have a gang, I created a character that represented the other side of the tracks—the kid who wasn't in high school."

. . . And here he flags the start of the race.
© by Paramount Pictures Corporation

The car, an integral part of the Fifties, is brought into "Happy Days" via the drag race episode. Here, Fonzie counsels Richie, one of the participants in the race. © by Paramount Pictures Corporation

Now, in partnership with executive producers Tom Miller and Ed Milkis, who had worked on the original pilot in a different capacity, Marshall began revising. In addition to introducing a modified gang element (Fonzie, of course), he redesigned Arnold's and added many more kids.

The inclusion of cars in "Happy Days" was another area of development. *American Graffiti* provided a model in this respect also. The emphasis on cars was pronounced in the Fifties. Marshall knew that, having lived through it, and recognized the authenticating value to the show, as well as the thematic value, of the car. This adjustment, however, meant bringing the show outdoors more often, which in turn meant losing some of the comedic control. It was a compromise, one of several in the evolution of the show. Later, according to Marshall, after the series' first season, the network would tell him to bring "Happy Days" back indoors to beef up the humor.

"Outside you can get nice pictures," he explains. "Indoors you can be funnier. But you can't have both. It's just too expensive to put it together."

Thematically, Marshall's intent was clear in his mind from the beginning. While many believed (and still do) that "Happy Days" is essentially a work of nostalgia, it never really has been. Under the superficial Fifties elements, Marshall wanted to explore and reflect on the pain of adolescence. In fact, the nostalgic aspect of the show can be seen as incidental—frills, if you will, that give the show an immediately observable identity. Aside from Marshall's interest in the period, setting the show in the Fifties was actually convenient. In a sense, the Fifties element was a way to develop the theme accurately while avoiding aspects of modern youth that would be necessary for realism but hard for the network, and presumably the audience, to swallow. Marshall explains:

"It's very hard to do a show about young people on TV without showing marijuana or needles or things of that nature that are unacceptable. When people see a show about modern kids without those elements, they simply say, 'That's not true.' The thing about the Fifties is you can do a show about young people without getting into that area. That was calculated. The same applies to sex. When Richie says he's just going to kiss a girl goodnight, the audience buys it because the morality was different then."

Two basic male adolescent pains were focused on in developing the show's

The pain of growing up. Even Fonzie can't totally escape it. © by Paramount Pictures Corporation

Even politics enters into "Happy Days." As the campaign fever heats up, the guys take time out to do a little girl-watching. © *by Paramount Pictures Corporation*

theme. The first has to do with girls; hence Richie's, Potsie's and Ralph's never-ending quest for dates and Fonzie's never-ending role as the guru of dating technique. The second pain revolves around the question "Am I a coward?"

"This always comes up when someone's going to hit you," Marshall says. "I had many of those feelings as a young man. I was in with the toughs but I wasn't really tough myself. You were constantly called upon to prove that you were a man. And that's very painful."

In one episode the pain theme is even brought into the character of Howard Cunningham as he comes to terms with middle age on his forty-fifth birthday.

"Happy Days," says Marshall, is based on the Lenny Bruce formula—pain plus time equals comedy. Although adult interest in the show came as something of a surprise to the producers, it could have been predicted. Following the Lenny Bruce formula, it's not hard to see how adults, separated from their adolescence by a sea of time, can view "Happy Days," recall their growing pains, and laugh at what can now be seen as humorous.

Fonzie delivers a pro-Eisenhower speech to the Junior Citizens. It just so happens most of the chicks are backing Ike.
© by Paramount Pictures Corporation

He's not the tall, bully type but he can do it with his eyes and his voice. And I can't find anyone who can do it with his eyes and his voice." It was Henry Winkler.

Marshall knew and trusted Miller. The excitement soon became mutual. When Marshall saw Winkler, he was quickly convinced. What Miller had told him was true. Henry Winkler was the perfect Fonzie.

Only the roles of Joanie and Marion Cunningham were to prove trouble-free. Marion Ross was ideal and Erin Moran had worked with Marshall before. His logic here was simple. "She was funny then and she'll probably be funny now. And she was."

Eventually, the course of episodes would break down into three categories. The "Fonzie-hero" show, the "family" show, and the "examination" show. Of the last category, notable examples are Richie's questioning of yellow journalism, Fonzie's examination of marriage, and Richie's conflict between supporting Adlai Stevenson for President and upholding his family's pro-Eisenhower stance—a unique political/comedy blend.

With theme and story plots conceived, Marshall turned his attention to casting. Given wide responsibility in this area, Tom Miller approached Marshall one day with the solution to what was beginning to become a problem—casting Fonzie. Miller was excited. "I've got a guy," he told Marshall. "He's not quite what your image is.

"I like Ike . . . and my bike likes Ike."
© by Paramount Pictures Corporation

Ron Howard was also familiar to Marshall all the way back to "The Andy Griffith Show." In Marshall's eyes, Howard had the

Ronnie Howard, a familiar face in show business, pedals around the Paramount lot. Marshall liked Howard for the role of Richie Cunningham for the very reason doubt existed in the minds of others—he wasn't the superstar type. © by Paramount Pictures Corporation

unique capability of representing something very American while having the potential to be very funny. Although at one point there was some doubt about casting him because he wasn't a super-hero, it was just that quality, his being "a nice kid," that made him well-suited for the part. Be-

sides, at age nineteen, Howard was a veteran and, in Marshall's words, "a solid actor."

For the role of Potsie Weber, Marshall was going in large part for a dark-haired actor to contrast with red-haired Ron Howard. Other than that, he wanted a "pleasant kid who could get a laugh." Again Tom Miller had a candidate. Anson Williams was screen tested (a test that was "somewhat rigged" by Marshall to stave off network doubts about Williams), and although his acting credits weren't the most impressive, Williams worked so well with Ron Howard that he got the role.

But another young actor had been very impressive in his bid for the Potsie role. One strike against him, no doubt, was his red hair. Not quite right for the part, Donny Most had proved, however, to be "a very funny guy." Marshall gave it some thought—Most could be a decided asset to the show. What followed was perhaps one of the greatest testimonials to the actor's relatively unknown talent. Marshall created the role of Ralph Malph specifically for Donny Most.

The biggest problem was casting Howard Cunningham. Harold Gould had taken the original part in the first pilot but he was off working on another project. According to Marshall, the network was adamant in its desire for a "Father Knows Best" image for Howard Cunningham. But Marshall was equally firm in sticking to his original notion of Howard Cunningham as a vulnerable, real-life father.

"This wonderful man who knows all the answers just wouldn't work," Marshall still maintains. "I know where you can get a laugh—and I knew we couldn't get a laugh out of that stereotype.

"So I said, 'In all honesty I don't recall my father being such a genius while I was growing up and I'd like a father that the audience can relate to, someone who doesn't look like a giant!'"

In the meantime, Marshall and Miller came up with Tom Bosley—the epitome of Howard Cunningham, but the antithesis of the network's concept.

"The network said, 'No, you can't have Tom Bosley,'" Marshall recalls. "They

Tom Bosley's ability to portray Howard Cunningham as a normal, vulnerable father was just right for the part. Here, Howard handles a somewhat tipsy Richie in very sympathetic, unpretentious manner. © by Paramount Pictures Corporation

said, 'He doesn't look like a father, he looks like MY father.' But that's exactly what we wanted."

The conflict raged and, of course, Marshall triumphed—something for which he still counts his blessings. For not only does Bosley unfalteringly portray the character, he also gives a degree of stability to a cast that may be mature beyond its years in professionalism and strength, but is young in chronological years, nevertheless.

"You need a veteran in there to solidify the work," Marshall contends. "When I first met Tom I was impressed by his togetherness as a person. When you do a series week after week after week, you need this kind of stability.

"Ronnie is very stable, but he's still pretty young. We need a rock and that's what Tom is. He's helped us over some rough periods."

Sets and costumes also proved troublesome. Extensive research was undertaken to insure authenticity (including frequent runs on local garage sales). But although money was a problem, the biggest obstacle was geography. Born and raised in New York City, Marshall could easily have constructed "Happy Days" on his own turf. But instead he opted for Milwaukee, Tom Miller's home town. It was unique—nobody had used Milwaukee as the setting for a show—and it was an East/West compromise.

Marshall had hired his writers from both coasts and, of course, Miller was the midground. But arguments arose immediately because the surface elements of the Fifties varied according to location. The effort eventually was toward compromise—use a little from here and a little from there, with the obvious result being a hodge-podge of nostalgia that at no time existed all at once and in the same place.

Letters still come to the "Happy Days" offices criticizing this no-man's-land of nostalgia, but the trend has declined as the audience presumably shifts its focus from the setting to the characters—proof that the smash popularity of "Happy Days" isn't hinging on its Fifties setting.

At last, some three years after the creation of the original pilot, "Happy Days" went into production. With an unwavering vigor that was to become a way of life for the cast, producers, writers, and crew, a

This one was snapped in 1975.
© by Paramount Pictures Corporation

One of the first group publicity photos of the "Happy Days" guys. This one was taken in 1974.
© by Paramount Pictures Corporation

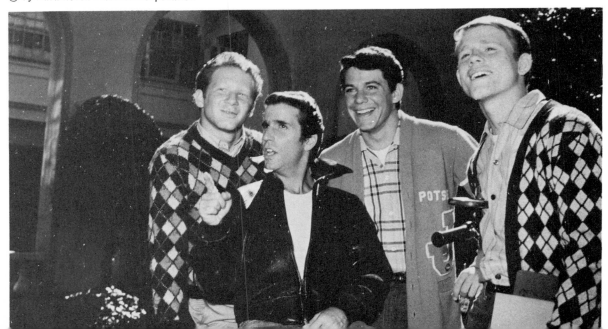

string of sixteen episodes to be aired in the second half of the 1973–74 television season was begun. As mentioned before, it was a young cast and that might have been anticipated to be a source of immediate problems. But, according to Marshall, something far more basic proved to be the trouble spot in these earliest days.

Although ABC-TV had been the source of the idea of bringing the gang element into "Happy Days," once Fonzie was developed and brought into the show's stories, the network, says Marshall, balked. Coming from a largely gang-oriented background, Marshall knew that the Fifties hood derived much of his power through silence. That power even went beyond the axiom "actions speak louder than words," although that was a part of it. Simply put, a few well-chosen words or expressions could carry infinitely more clout than a long harangue.

Evidence of Marshall's desire to impute this trait to his "gang representative" can be seen in the first episode, when Fonzie had only six lines.

But ABC-TV didn't like it one bit, says Marshall. The tough guy had become too tough. In addition to the fact that there was very little of a redeeming nature in the character of the original Fonzie, the problem basically went back to the principle underlying the hassle over Bosley. Fonzie was too real.

After writing the "flagship" episode, Marshall went off to Hawaii to work on "The Odd Couple," leaving Bob Brunner, head script writer and an old friend, on the set "to keep everything honest." When Marshall returned, he found Fonzie in a windbreaker and loafers, looking not unlike the other characters. Marshall was shocked, to say the least, and immediately consulted Brunner, who told him, "The network's been driving me crazy."

Winkler also expressed his dismay. Hav-

ing been given a certain degree of latitude in developing his role, Winkler was now concerned that Fonzie was being ruined through the subtle modifications in his personality and appearance.

"I went to the network and had a fit," Marshall recalls. "I simply told them that the character was being destroyed. 'Why, ' I asked, 'would anyone wear a windbreaker on a motorcycle? You'd freeze to death.' "

ABC gave in, according to Marshall, but with the stipulation that Fonzie wear the leather jacket only when on his motorcycle. The result was that whenever Fonzie appeared in a scene, so did his bike.

Another Fonzie-related problem also arose at this time, but the settlement, in the long run, was beneficial for all involved. The disagreement again revolved around Marshall's attempt to recreate Fonzie in the image of the true Fifties hood and the network's desire to temper this hard-core, perhaps unpleasant, personality.

Of the many peculiarities that characterized the Fifties tough, perhaps his paradoxical sense of right and wrong is the most distinguishing. Not unlike modern-day gang members, the Fifties hood embraced a strange code that appears contradictory to the middle-class American. Prepared to do bodily harm for what might appear unfounded reasons (the phrase "I don't like your face" comes to mind as an example), the gang member of the Fifties vehemently upheld the tradition of God, mother, and country. At once, such unbridled hoods embodied the irrational fighter and the keeper of the American way of life.

This was to be the essence of Fonzie's value system, God, mother, and country being his "good side."

"The problem was that ABC wanted him to have a wider morality," Marshall explains. "They wanted him to do things like help the Cunninghams once in a while.

"So there was a compromise. Instead of seeing Fonzie punch somebody, we'd just talk about it. And he would eventually come to help the Cunninghams and the boys."

Henry, Ron, and Anson in costume take a break during the filming of one of the first episodes. Notice that even though he's on his bike, Fonzie wears a windbreaker, not his trademark leather jacket. © by Paramount Pictures Corporation

In January, 1974, the first episode of "Happy Days" was aired. Throughout the industry there had been some speculation that the show was doomed from the beginning, due largely to its unfavorable time slot. Pitted against "Maude" and "Adam-12," "Happy Days" certainly seemed to be facing an uphill battle.

Despite the odds, Tom Bosley was optimistic before the show debuted. "I feel viewers are ready for a well-done, strictly entertaining show that they can just sit

Even in a courtroom scene, the lighthearted nature of "Happy Days" comes through. Not exactly courtroom duds on The Fonz.
© by Paramount Pictures Corporation

"Good Times" suddenly burst on the scene carried largely by J. J. Walker. Walker proved more of an opponent than "Maude," and "Good Times," punched up to the hilt with big-joke humor and Walker's effervescent character, quickly overtook "Happy Days."

It had been a hectic, often bedazzling, year for "Happy Days." In the short half-season, the show had triumphed and been conquered. But all was not lost. Marshall readily admits that because the show aired in mid-season, preparations were less than desirable and some of the shows, as a result, "a little ragged."

Their work was clear-cut. "Happy Days" simply had to get funnier if it was to stand up to "Good Times." Two major changes were effected in this vein. First, adhering to the principle that humor can best be

Fonzie takes the stand.
© by Paramount Pictures Corporation

back and enjoy and forget the anxieties they run into everywhere else," he said.

His anticipations proved correct. "Happy Days" made noise immediately, easily outdistancing "Adam-12" from its first week on the air. The battle narrowed to "Happy Days" vs. "Maude" with the tables turning from week to week based on as little as one rating point of difference. Unquestionably, "Happy Days" was faring against "Maude" better than any other show ever had.

Still in the first half-season, however, CBS decided to move "Maude" to another time slot and replace the show with one that could compete with "Happy Days" on essentially the same ground, simultaneously freeing Maude to dominate her new spot.

controlled indoors, Marshall revised the show's format and brought it onto stage sets.

Second, "Happy Days" started filming before a live audience. The strategy is a simple one. Actors perform better before an audience than they do facing only a camera lens, and the writers, through both audience pressure and feedback, are compelled to write funnier.

The new direction worked. In its second season (actually its first *full* season) "Happy Days" slowly began to climb the ratings ladder until it caught up with and surpassed "Good Times" and eventually the whole time slot.

According to Marshall, ABC was still concerned that Fonzie was too tough, but the show was flying and there wasn't a whole lot they could say.

Henry, Anson, and Ron take a break next to the "Barbary Coast" set.
© by Paramount Pictures Corporation

In this early 1974 photo, Anson seems to be giving Henry an impression of where he and "Happy Days" are going.
© by Paramount Pictures Corporation

It wasn't until the third season, though, that things really began happening. All of a sudden, Fonzie—the one-time thorn in ABC-TV's side—had worked his way into the hearts of "Happy Days" fans and had, in fact, become the focal point of their interest in the show. Everyone knew it and ABC-TV wanted more of what had gone from a very sensitive thing to a very good thing. It wasn't hard to figure that Fonzie would get even bigger come the third season, and with him "Happy Days."

The word came down from the network: "Give us more Fonzie."

Undoubtedly, Marshall had a strong affinity for this burgeoning character. Not only had he grown up with Fonzie's real-life counterparts, but he had already had to struggle to maintain the character's integrity. Marshall's creative sense, however, was stronger than his sentimentality. Fonzie was never meant to be a primary figure in "Happy Days," although his personality had become crucial to both the show's theme and its level of humor. And an increased emphasis on the darling-hood simply didn't fit into Marshall's scheme of story plots for the third season. But Marshall had to concede.

As he had done so often before, the man at the helm of "Happy Days" began the trying process of reworking the show's format. The problem was obvious—how to increase the presence of a character that is not often close to the immediate setting. It was basically a tactical question, one that had to be answered for the sake of the writers who would ultimately be responsible for carrying the change through.

The solution was to move Fonzie into the Cunningham's garage apartment in the first episode of the third season. Marshall was still dissatisfied that Fonzie—originally cast as a silent-menace type—would now not only appear more often, but would speak more often as well. The consolation was, of course, that "Happy Days" was doing well and if perpetuating and increasing the success meant more Fonzie . . . so be it.

In this same vein, one other development had to be dealt with. Through extensive research, Marshall discovered that the "Happy Days" audience was beginning to respond to Fonzie more as a hero than as a tough guy. Again adjustments had to be made—mostly in Fonzie's actions. If the audience wanted a hero, Fonzie needed a vehicle to achieve heroism. And the vehicle turned out literally to be a vehicle—his motorcycle. The "Fearless Fonzarelli" episode, in which Fonzie undertakes a record "garbage can jump" on his bike, was conceived. Interestingly, it is Fonzie's fear that he is losing his cool that motivates

him to delve into the "Evel Knievel Syndrome." Consistent with the "Happy Days" theme, Fonzie's heroism in this episode ultimately stems from pain—from another of the questions with which even the coolest of the cool is confronted during adolescence: "Am I cool?"

The recent history of "Happy Days" is well known and in great part revolves around the "Fonzie cult," not an unknown phenomenon by any means. At its peak, "Happy Days" was scoring Nielsen rating points of 29 with a 43 share. This means that of all television sets, whether on or off, 29 percent were tuned into "Happy Days" at that particular time and that of those sets actually turned on, 43 per cent were tuned into "Happy Days"—an excellent achievement by all standards. During the 1975–76 season, "Happy Days" was eclipsed by none other than its sister series "Laverne and Shirley," which means little considering that "Laverne and Shirley" was rated number one and "Happy Days" number two.

The ratings, however, don't tell nearly the whole story. The show's success can be measured in many ways that are more telling. For instance, there were the recurring rumors in late 1975 that Henry Winkler was dead. Despite our desire to believe that such rumors are produced in the sardonic offices of publicity mills, the fact is that their conception, dissemination, and acceptance are factors of the audience's desperate fear of losing its heroes.

And the fan mail. According to Jack Tamkin and Tom Bishop, the two men responsible for handling "Happy Days" fan mail, some 60,000 letters come in per month—most of them addressed to Winkler. In relation to other television shows past and present, the volume of "Happy

Although Garry Marshall claims the "Happy Days" gang doesn't go out too much together, they have organized a league softball team. Here, Mighty Henry connects with the ball.
Photo by Ben Davidson

Days" and Winkler/Fonzie fan mail is considered very high.

Further proof that "Happy Days," and particularly Fonzie, has become at least a temporary institution in our nation is the vast merchandising effort capitalizing on Fonzie . . . $5 Fonzie T-shirts, $2-a-pair Fonzie knee socks, $30 Fonzie jackets, posters, buttons, thermoses—the list goes on and on. Rarely since the Davy Crockett craze that netted businessmen millions in the mid-Fifties has the market been flooded with such cult merchandise.

Add to this the waiting list of 5,000 to see the "Happy Days" filmings and the personal success of the show's stars (especially Winkler and Anson Williams) since the inception of "Happy Days," even the popularity of the "Happy Days" theme song, and the picture becomes clear.

How long can this last? "I think we definitely have another two years, giving us a total of five," says Marshall. "We'll move the kids up into college and probably do more Fonzie hero things because that can last for years.

"The reason I say five years is that I've worked enough shows to know that after five years the cast gets a little punchy. The networks don't like to hear that but it's a fact of life."

Five years. Will that be enough? Audiences are notoriously fickle. Maybe it will prove too much. From where we stand right now, though, that doesn't seem likely. Although Marshall notes that they "don't go out together like some other casts purport to do," he is glad to note that the entire staff works well and enjoyably together.

Ron Howard, for one, agrees with that. "We all seemed to hit it off together from the first time we met. We had fun doing the show, and I just felt those who watched would find it fun too."

Is there any question about that?

Henry toes the rubber and goes into his wind-up.
Photo by Ben Davidson

3

Notes on The Fonz: An Interview with Garry Marshall

Notes on The Fonz:
An Interview with Garry Marshall

Q. When you realized you needed a gang representative in the "Happy Days" concept, what did you draw on in creating Fonzie?

A. I grew up in the Bronx and was a member of The Falcons, one of the forty-eight or so gangs around the area at that time. The Falcons got caught up in the wave of sports when the police gave up trying to stop gangs from fighting and gave them baseball bats and gloves (which, by the way, was part of the "Fonzie the Flatfoot" episode). I use a lot of my own experiences in developing Fonzie and "Happy Days" in general.

Q. Were there any members of The Falcons upon whom Fonzie is based?

A. Oh yes. There was a guy named Roger (who's now in prison) who was totally unpredictable. You never knew what he was going to do from one minute to the next. He could be a very nice guy and then suddenly hit somebody. It was very hard to figure out what was going to make him lose his temper. We do that a lot with Fonzie.

There was another guy named Carmine who I used in "Laverne and Shirley." He was just the toughest guy in the neighborhood. He'd do things like pull a car with

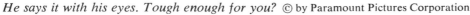

He says it with his eyes. Tough enough for you? © by Paramount Pictures Corporation

Fonzie the elder—wiser and more worldly—is the guys' guide into unconquered worlds.
© by Paramount Pictures Corporation

his teeth. He was older than the rest of us, out of school, and working in a shoeshine shop. I added that older quality to Fonzie also.

Q. Why was that necessary?

A. When I developed Fonzie, I was trying to get a guy who had dropped out of school and was older than Richie and the others so he could be not only tougher, but more worldly.

Q. What about the violent quality that seems so much a part of toughness?

A. I didn't use the part about zip guns and all the other things we used to do in The Falcons because Fonzie had to fit into the TV framework. Instead, I took Fonzie to be the guy who was in The Falcons, but now it's all over. He's past that stage and gone to work.

He's not the guy in *American Graffiti*. He's out of the gang, although in one episode he did go back to see the Falcons. Fonzie's in the middle place—an uneducated guy trying to make a living. His gang days are over. The only carry-over is that he keeps going out with girls, working on cars, and riding his bike and wearing a leather jacket.

Q. How did you arrive at the name Fonzie?

A. I remember the night we were writing the final version of the script and I said "I need a rough Italian" but I didn't have the name. I thought of calling him Carmine Ragusa because we always used to call him "The Big Ragu." But that didn't quite fit.

At that time, a friend of mine from New York who was working with me on "The

Little People"—that was Bob Brunner—came up with the name Arthur Fonzarelli. His point was that we would have a lot of different ways to go with that name—Fonzie or The Fonz.

Q. How has Henry Winkler influenced Fonzie?

A. Henry has had a lot to do with developing Fonzie. Most of the mannerisms were created by him. For instance, he added the "Aaaayyy" to a simple "Hey" in the dialogue. Another example: at one point he goes into the bathroom and looks into the mirror to comb his hair. He brings the comb up to his head, looks at himself and without combing at all he says, "Aaayyy." Now that was Henry. A lot of character development is done on stage.

Q. The Fonz, usually considered an idol of cool, has become somewhat of a sex symbol as well. Was that intentional?

A. In a sense it was intentional and goes back to the idea of the theme of "Happy Days" being the pain of growing up. One of those pains involves girls and not being able to make it with them like Fonzie does.

So if Richie's problem is that he's not good with girls, which was of course calculated, then there has to be somebody in his life who is dynamite with them to make the pain more pronounced. Fonzie is awesome to the other characters in his power over women.

Q. He's also a bit of a male chauvinist. Do you think women find that offensive?

A. Henry plays Fonzie with a macho attitude that also includes excellent comedy timing. So Fonzie, even as a total chauvinist, doesn't offend women because they know it's a joke and as a result they get into the macho thing and find him very sexy. Besides, Henry *is* sexy.

Q. Don't you find it amazing that Fonzie has appeal both for kids and adults?

A. One of my favorite things is *Gulliver's Travels* because I like stories that work on

two levels. Fonzie works on two levels in that respect. To a certain younger level of audience, Fonzie is real—he's Superman. They believe in Superman and they believe in Fonzie.

I think the adult element takes him with a grain of salt like he's putting them on a little, and so they can enjoy him and laugh.

Q. Why did you begin to lean so heavily on Fonzie even though "Happy Days" was doing well?

A. It's kind of hard to say. Our ratings were good but not good enough. We were looking to be more competitive and Fonzie was our most competitive character.

Basically, we needed something to compete with J. J. on "Good Times." Richie couldn't balance off J. J. because they just aren't in the same world. So we decided to push Fonzie.

He became more and more popular and when you have a popular character you push him. But it had nothing to do with somebody being able to act better than somebody else. It was purely competitive.

Q. When do you think the Fonzie craze really began?

"Off the bed, Malph."
© by Paramount Pictures Corporation

A. The turning point in the show was the motorcycle jump episode. That's what got people talking about the character—not twenty million but forty million. It didn't get the highest ratings but those who watched talked about it to everyone else and at that point the show began to rise. It was basically conceived as a hype to bring attention to the show in the middle of the season.

Q. Do you think the focus on Fonzie has in any way degraded "Happy Days"—at least your original concept of the show?

A. I don't think so. In twenty-two episodes we're going to cover all the bases I wanted to cover. There are some people judging from the mail, not many but some and mostly adults, who preferred the softer version of the family.

In their minds the emphasis on Fonzie is

This photo and those on the following pages in this chapter chronicle one of the first steps toward Fonzie's role as hero. Here Potsie and Ralph try to tempt an unwilling Fonzie to sing at the senior dance. © *by Paramount Pictures Corporation*

It doesn't look like Ralph and Potsie have been too successful. © *by Paramount Pictures Corporation*

degrading to the show. They're entitled to think that, so every once in a while we give them the "Potsie-love" kind of show—the warm kind of thing to balance it off. To appeal to everybody is to appeal to nobody, but we try to provide this balance.

Q. But what about things like the audience wildly cheering when Fonzie makes an entrance?

A. We used to take the cheering for Fonzie out, but because of the competition, to enhance the excitement of the show, we decided to leave this spontaneous thing on the track. We never add it in.

What we do now is introduce the cast before the actual filming so the audience doesn't go completely wild. The other night Howard even got a big hand.

Q. How has the increased focus on Fonzie affected the role of Richie Cunningham?

A. Well, we do lean heavily on Fonzie, there's no question about that. But we depend a lot on Fonzie-Richie stories too. In the 1976–77 season, we'll do some Richie stories, some Fonzie stories and a lot of Fonzie-Richie stories.

The Fonzie character works better when it has Richie to play off. We found that out when Ronnie left to do his movie. We were left with Fonzie alone and it just didn't work as well.

The chemistry is better when Henry can play off Ronnie.

We call Ronnie "The Bob Cousy of Comedy" because he can feed and also score when he has to. It's hard to find that kind of actor in comedy.

Q. In that same vein, were there any intra-cast problems when you began to push Fonzie?

A. In coming to terms with the emphasis on Fonzie, I'm sure all the actors had to come to grips with their egos. But the bottom line was survival, and even though we were never doing that bad, there was some fear of cancellation.

The cast and crew liked the "Happy Days" situation and each other and thought "Gee, it would be a shame if this went off the air because we're having fun." So when we moved to Fonzie, I think everyone decided that if this is what's going to keep us going, then it's all right and that's what we'll have to do.

I think Ronnie's being a very mature person for his age also helped him deal with it. He knows the business and knows that it's better to be a hit than to not be.

Q. What, in your view, has Fonzie come to represent?

A. In the beginning I knew we needed a representative from the other side of the tracks, someone who everyone wanted to be like, not exactly like, but wanting some of his characteristics—mainly his coolness and power to resist being pushed around.

Finally pushed into it, Fonzie rehearses with the gang. © by Paramount Pictures Corporation

As Richie stands in confusion, holding Fonzie's costume, The Fonz has second thoughts about his gig.
© by Paramount Pictures Corporation

Now, I feel, the character represents, in a sense, a hero in a society that has none. He's become much more of a hero than I thought originally, but that's good. I think originally I was wrong. Joe DiMaggio was my hero and there aren't any more Joe DiMaggio's left. So I gave the audience one and they said, "Yeah, we need one of those", especially after Watergate.

I think he represents a hero easily identifiable, one that doesn't cause anxiety. As a hero, he can say things and people listen.

At last . . . it's The Fonz—fullblown.
© by Paramount Pictures Corporation

© by Paramount Pictures Corporation

When he said wearing glasses is cool, we got a ton of mail from parents saying "Thank you for saying that; my son was so embarrassed and now he's happy."

So I think on one level, the character can do some good. He's a hero the country is welcoming and he's also a character that can get a laugh and entertain.

Henry says something about the character I agree with. "Fonzie represents someone who won't be pushed around in a time in history when many people are being pushed around."

Q. But can people really identify with him?

A. People say the key to TV is to present characters the audience can totally identify with. I don't think that's true. A very successful show today is one in which there's somebody the audience can identify with, and that's Richie. But there's a need for a character that the audience can't identify with at all but would like to be like.

That's what people want to see—somebody who they're not like but would like to be like. That's why they'll go for "The Bionic Woman." Who can identify with her?

The desire to be like someone else is one of the strongest emotions in any audience. I think Fonzie brings that emotion out in a large amount of people.

4

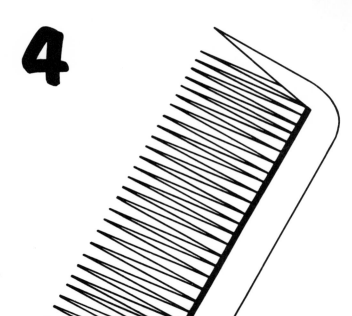

The Cast

HENRY WINKLER
(Fonzie)

Henry Winkler

Several stage plays, two motion pictures, and guest appearances on the Mary Tyler Moore and Bob Newhart TV shows preceded Henry Winkler's selection for his role in "Happy Days" and his quick leap into stardom.

Henry was born in New York City, son of Ilse and Harry Winkler, both of whom fled Nazi Germany to come to the United States in 1939.

For years, Henry was expected to take over his father's lucrative lumber exporting firm, but even during his early years, he had other ideas.

In the eighth grade, Henry played Billy Budd. A few years later he did Wintergreen in "Of Thee I Sing," his first musical, in the eleventh grade at the McBurney School for Boys in New York. He says he never hoped to become anything but an actor.

During high school and college, Henry spent four months of several different years studying in Lausanne, Switzerland, and working in a lumber mill in a small German town. He was graduated from Emerson College in Boston as a drama major with emphasis also on child psychology.

If he hadn't succeeded as an actor, he believes he would have become a child psychologist. He is still deeply interested in helping children in need.

"I'm still very interested in children and in trying to help the underprivileged, needy, or in-trouble ones. I try to make as many appearances before them as possible," he remarks.

In 1967, Henry represented Emerson at the Yale School of Drama Festival in a play, *Donner*, about the Donner Pass tragedy. Influenced by the director, Thomas B. Hass, he began concentrating on drama rather than the musicals that had concerned him most while at Emerson.

After Emerson, Henry entered the Yale School of Drama and earned his Master of Fine Arts degree, appearing in more than thirty plays as a student. Upon graduation, he remained with the Yale company for a year and a half as a professional member.

Next, he joined the Arena Theatre in Washington, D.C., where he lasted just three weeks. "I was fired, the first time in my life—a mind-boggling experience," he recalls.

In New York, he began getting work in radio and TV commercials, appeared in the NET programs "The Great American Dream Machine" and "Masquerade," and then

toured with the Children's Story Theatre, receiving $19 per performance.

With a group of friends, Henry next put together an evening of improvisations, "Off the Wall," presented off-Broadway.

That was followed by his first motion picture, *Lords of Flatbush*. Next came a Broadway play, *42 Seconds from Broadway*, followed by another stage production, *In-*

© by Paramount Pictures Corporation

cident at Vichy, in Cincinnati, and a second film, *Crazy Joe*.

After considerable persuasion from his agent, Henry left New York for California in September, 1973. During the following month, he landed guest roles in the Mary Tyler Moore and Bob Newhart shows and, on his birthday, his role in "Happy Days."

Two months after the first "Happy Days" episode had aired, Henry walked out of a TV studio to find several hundred young girls lined up awaiting him.

He still can't believe his instant success.

"It's mind-blowing," he says. "And to think, I said 'No' the first time my agent tried to get me to come to Hollywood. I'm lucky he was persistent."

More recently, Henry has starred in the TV film "Katherine," and in a stage produc-duction of *Room Service* in Ohio. He has also appeared at several concerts and on "The Dinah Shore Show." Considering himself a serious actor rather than a stand-up comedian, however, he has shied away from variety shows.

A bachelor, Henry lives in a modest house in the Hollywood hills and says he is a strong believer in the family and intends one day to have his own.

"One of the aspects of 'Happy Days' that appeals to me most is its strong emphasis on the close family life that existed in the Fifties," Henry says.

"That doesn't hold true so much today," he adds. "Young people, I find, often don't quite know where to go."

VITAL STATISTICS

Birthday: October 30
Birthplace: New York City
Height: 5'6½"
Weight: 134 lbs.
Hair: Brown
Eyes: Hazel

RON HOWARD
(Richie Cunningham)

Ron Howard

One of the best-known young actors of our time, Ron Howard finds himself at the peak of his career following a long series of successes.

Ron didn't waste any time getting started with his career. He was two years old when he made his stage debut at Baltimore's Hilltop Theatre, appearing with his parents Rance and Jean Howard in *The Seven Year Itch.*

He had barely turned four when he joined Yul Brynner and Deborah Kerr in Vienna, Austria, to appear with them in *The Journey,* his first motion picture.

After *The Journey,* Ron experienced the only "dry spell" of his career.

"It lasted nine months and convinced me I really wanted to act," he says. "I still feel that way, although now I know that I also want to do more—and I want someday to write, direct, and produce."

Ron was still four when his first Hollywood job marked his television bow on "The Red Skelton Show."

Prior to "Happy Days," he was a regular on two other series. For eight years, he co-starred on "The Andy Griffith Show" as Andy's son, Opie. For two seasons, in 1970 and 1971, he was co-starred with Henry Fonda in "The Smith Family."

Ron was born in Duncan, Oklahoma. Six weeks later, he and his mother joined his father at Chanute Air Force Base, Illinois, where Rance Howard was stationed. Ron was introduced to backstage theatrical life when he was two months old, his parents being active with USO shows and Special Services productions.

When his father completed his Air Force hitch, the family moved to Baltimore, where Ron shortly was to make his start in acting. One reviewer wrote, "He was on stage less than a minute, but, during that time opening night, he stole the show."

After his TV debut on "The Red Skelton Show," Ron kept busy with roles on three "Playhouse 90" productions, a second Skelton program, five "Dennis the

Menace" episodes, four segments of "The Many Loves of Dobie Gillis," and appearances on "Five Fingers," "Twilight Zone," and "The Dinah Shore Show."

Ron was co-starring with Bert Lahr in a G.E. Theatre presentation of "Barnaby and Mr. O'Malley" when producer Sheldon Leonard saw him and cast him as Opie on "The Andy Griffith Show."

During hiatuses in its long run, he played Winthrop Paroo in the movie *The Music Man*, co-starred with Glenn Ford as Eddie in *The Courtship of Eddie's Father*, and made TV guest appearances on "The Fugitive," "Dr. Kildare," "Big Valley," "Route 66," "I Spy," "The Danny Kaye Show," "Gomer Pyle, USMC," and "The Monroes."

After "The Andy Griffith Show," he guest-starred on such series as "The F.B.I.," "Daniel Boone," "Gentle Ben," "Gunsmoke," and two Disney two-part dramas, "A Boy Called Nuthin' " and "Smoke."

More recently, Ron has had guest spots on several Dinah Shore shows, "The Rich Little Show," "The Waltons," and the PBS production, "I'm a Fool."

In addition to starring in *American Graffiti*, Ron has had leading roles in Disney's *Wild Country* and *Eat My Dust*, and recently co-starred with John Wayne in *The Shootist*.

Other motion picture credits include *Mother's Day, Harry Spikes, Huck Finn*, and simultaneously with "Happy Days," the TV special "The Migrants" and the TV movie "Locusts."

On June 7, 1975, while on vacation from "Happy Days" filming, Ron was married to his longtime sweetheart, Cheryl Alley.

Ron has studied cinema arts at the University of Southern California, but as a result of landing his "Happy Days" role, he was forced to withdraw. Although he had planned to return to college, the success of the series makes that unfeasible.

"I'm afraid I'll have to limit myself to a few night or correspondence courses and not take on too heavy a load," Ron says. "It looks like it'll take quite a few years for me to graduate."

Basketball and baseball are Ron's favorite sports, and in fact, despite his many acting chores, he even found time to star on his high school basketball team.

It was his determination to make his prep hoop team that once caused him to turn down two tempting roles—a choice his parents left up to him.

Although his career has been rigorous and time-consuming, Ron doesn't feel he's missed anything in growing up.

"My parents saw to it that I went to public schools and had time to enter into sports. Rather than missing anything, I gained a lot—meeting different people, going different places, learning an understanding of work responsibility and a skill that is enjoyable to me."

Ron also enjoys swimming, skating, bowling, tennis and hiking. Photography is a pet hobby, and he once won second place in Kodak's national teenage one-reeler home movie contest.

VITAL STATISTICS

Birthday: March 1
Birthplace: Duncan, Okla.
Height: 5'9"
Weight: 145
Hair: Red
Eyes: Hazel

ANSON WILLIAMS
(Potsie Weber)

"Happy Days" has skyrocketed Anson Williams into recognition as one of the nation's most popular young actors.

Revealing his confidence and ambition, Anson says, "I believe I'm a good performer. I love acting, I like playing comedy as in "Happy Days," and I like doing variety shows where I can sing and dance."

Anson is an accomplished clarinet player and singer and also writes songs.

The decision to add music to "Happy Days" was a dream come true for Anson, who has recorded four songs of the Fifties as well as two new tunes which he has written.

Anson was born in Los Angeles and graduated from Burbank High School, rival school of John Burroughs High attended at the same time by Ron Howard.

Anson then enrolled at California State College, where his singing and acting talents were first developed.

"Growing up in Burbank in a non-show-business family, everything came together for me when I took a theatre arts course to round out my college schedule," Anson recalls.

"I discovered the magic that can happen between a performer and an audience, and I know there can't be a greater feeling than the one I get every time I'm on stage."

Working part-time jobs selling shoes,

versions of *Everyday People* and *Broadway a la Carte.*

These were followed by an appearance with Patti Andrews in *Victory Canteen* at the Ivar Theatre in Hollywood. Sighted by a talent agent, he began a string of thirty-two TV commercials.

One of those was the original MacDonald's commercial made in 1972. In it, Anson was shown leaping over a counter singing, "You deserve a break today . . ."

Leading up to his role in "Happy Days," he made increasingly prominent TV guest appearances on "Marcus Welby, M.D.," two episodes of "Owen Marshall, Counselor at Law," "The Paul Lynde Show," three variety specials with Tony Randall, and the Hallmark Hall of Fame special, "Lisa, Bright and Dark."

Other dramatic credits were chalked up in the CBS-TV playhouse production of "Day Before Sunday."

Anson has also done a number of TV variety shows such as the Mike Douglas and Merv Griffin shows, and national telethons such as the Democratic telethon, the Easter Seals telethon, and hundreds of Cerebral Palsy telethons.

In addition to being a concert favorite, Anson also appears on numerous TV game shows, including "Password," "The $25,000 Pyramid," "Match Game," and "The Magnificent Marble Machine." He's also been signed as a regular on "The Hollywood Squares."

Besides acting and music, Anson's other interests include baseball, football, surfing, and ecology.

VITAL STATISTICS

Birthday: September 24
Birthplace: Los Angeles
Height: 5'10"
Weight: 144
Hair: Brown
Eyes: Blue

hamburgers, and newspapers at one time or another to pay for voice and acting lessons, Anson began buying the Hollywood entertainment trade papers and going to auditions.

His first professional jobs materialized swiftly, taking him to Wichita, Kansas, for summer stock roles in such productions as *The Music Man, The Sound of Music,* and *South Pacific,* staged for the Kenley Theatres circuit.

Next, in New Mexico and California nightclubs, he performed in abbreviated

DONNY MOST
(Ralph Malph)

Donny Most

Red-haired, freckle-faced Donny Most, a native of Brooklyn, went westward to Hollywood and virtually overnight became a television success with his role in "Happy Days."

Donny first became interested in acting when, as a third grader, he saw the motion picture *The Jolson Story*. When he was fifteen, he was introduced to the world of entertainment in a specialty review featuring youngsters, ages eleven to sixteen, presented at various hotels on the Catskills borscht circuit in New York state.

Soon after, he began a serious study of acting with drama coach Elinor Raab and at workshops in New York City. Then it wasn't long until he landed his first job, performing in a commercial. Later he was to do more than forty commercials.

Following graduation from Erasmus Hall in Brooklyn, Donny attended Lehigh University in Bethlehem, Pennsylvania, for three years as a business major, and performed in school theatricals.

Prior to starting his final year at Lehigh, he decided to vacation for the summer in

Hollywood, "to get my feet wet and make contacts that might help me after graduating."

He never has been able to get back to Lehigh, although he still hopes someday to finish his college education.

In Hollywood, he was picked for roles in "Room 222" and "Emergency." Then, as he was about to return East and to school, his agent persuaded him to remain in California, "just to see what might develop."

Almost immediately, he was summoned to Paramount, where he was interviewed and then screen tested for "Happy Days." Donny was a hit, and although he didn't get the part he tried out for, Potsie, executive producer Garry Marshall created the role of Ralph Malph especially for him.

Donny has been busy on the series ever since but has had time for personal appearances on tour and for guest-star roles in "Petrocelli," *Huck Finn*, and *Crazy Momma* with Cloris Leachman.

Donny says he hopes to develop as an actor to the point where he can play a variety of roles—in dramas and musicals as well as comedies.

He is also interested in singing and plans are underway for him to do his first recording.

Donny's interests include sports, particularly water skiing and swimming.

Donny's parents, Joyce and Bernard Most, and his older sister Randye Schaeffer are still living in New York City.

VITAL STATISTICS

Birthday: August 8
Birthplace: Brooklyn, N.Y.
Height: 5'10"
Weight: 145
Hair: Red
Eyes: Blue

TOM BOSLEY
(Howard Cunningham)

Tom Bosley

A veteran Hollywood motion picture actor, Tom Bosley leaped into Broadway stardom when he became the first actor to achieve the grand slam of New York theatrical awards—the Tony, Drama Critics, ANTA and Newspaper Guild—for his performance in the title role of the 1959 smash musical *Fiorello!*

Proving his success was no one-shot affair, he since has maintained a steady pace of stellar portrayals on the stage, in motion pictures, and on television.

Born in Chicago, Tom attended De Paul University following his Navy service. Midway through college, he gave up law as his goal and transferred to a radio school, bent on becoming a sports announcer.

But he soon changed course again, deciding he wanted to act.

After performing on radio and with midwestern stock companies for a period, he headed for New York. To sustain himself, he parked cars at Central Park's Tavern on the Green, clerked in a brokerage house, and checked hats at the famed Lindy's Restaurant.

His start in the New York theater arrived with the off-Broadway production of Jean Anouilh's *Thieves' Carnival* in 1955, the same year that is the setting for "Happy Days."

"Those were happy days for me," he now recalls. "Although my happiest may have been that marvelous period of 1937–40—that was about as free of tensions as any we've had.

"But my first New York show ran for six months, and was followed by another that lasted four months. I was making twenty dollars a week and spending thirty dollars, but I knew every morning, when I got up, that I was going to the theater.

"We played to full houses and had good reviews, most of which singled me out. Yes, they were exciting days for me."

Tom followed with a season of summer

stock in Pennsylvania and another in Dallas, then toured in *Gentlemen Prefer Blondes* with Marie Wilson. After more stock in Washington, D.C., he received the call from George Abbott that turned his life around.

More than 200 actors auditioned for the *Fiorello!* lead. Through three auditions, Tom thought he was trying out for the job of understudy. The morning after the show's opening on November 23, 1959, Bosley was a star.

Following the two-year run of *Fiorello!*, Tom appeared in *Nowhere to Go but Up*, co-starred with Kim Stanley in William Inge's *Natural Affection*, toured in the national company of *Luv!* and returned to Broadway to star in *The Education of H*y*m*a*n* K*a*p*l*a*n*.

Tom co-starred with Steve McQueen and Natalie Wood in his first motion picture, *Love with a Proper Stranger*, in 1963. His performance brought him the International Laurel Award from the motion picture exhibitors, as one of the ten most promising new film personalities.

Among his other motion pictures are *The World of Henry Orient, Divorce, American Style, Yours, Mine and Ours, The Secret War of Harry Frigg*, and, most recently, *Mixed Company*.

His television appearances also have been noteworthy—in the role of Teddy in "Arsenic and Old Lace," as Sen. George Norris in "Profiles in Courage," in Arthur Miller's "Focus," in the 1973 Christmas Special "Miracle on 34th Street," and in the NBC movie "The Last Survivors."

Besides guest-starring in many of the leading TV series in the last several years, Tom was co-starred in "The Sandy Duncan Show" and also is well-known as the voice of the father in the cartoon series "Wait Till Your Father Gets Home."

Tom married dancer Jean Eliot in 1962, following their meeting during the run of *Fiorello!* They and their daughter, born in 1966, live in Beverly Hills.

Tom is an avid reader, switching from fiction to nonfiction and from history to biography, between new scripts. He also plays golf and tennis, follows sports, and describes his main avocation as "spending time with my daughter. It's a joy to watch her grow up."

VITAL STATISTICS

Birthdate: October 1
Birthplace: Chicago, Ill.
Height: 5'8¾"
Weight: 213 lbs
Hair: Dark brown
Eyes: Hazel

MARION ROSS
(Marion Cunningham)

Marion Ross

Although her stellar career also has encompassed the Broadway stage and motion pictures, television has been Marion Ross' medium. She has appeared on more than 400 TV shows.

Marion attained her greatest Broadway success when she starred in *Edwin Booth*. In films, she has played key roles with most of the major male stars, including Clark Gable, Frank Sinatra, William Holden, Kirk Douglas, Dean Martin, and Cary Grant.

Her pictures range from *Operation Petticoat, Teacher's Pet,* and *Lust for Life* in the late Fifties to *Airport, Colossus: The Forbin Project,* and *Honkey* in more recent times.

She has guest-starred on nearly every leading TV series of the past several years, including "Mannix," "Ironside," "Hawaii Five-O," "Marcus Welby, M.D.," and, earlier, "The Untouchables," "Perry Mason," and "The Loretta Young Show."

Marion was born in the small Minnesota town of Albert Lea. As a child, she moved to Minneapolis, where she became a familiar figure around the theatre stage of the University of Minnesota. She was far too young to be a student, but she worked as a stagehand nevertheless, avidly soaking up the theatrical background.

When her family moved to San Diego, California, she was old enough to enroll in San Diego State College. As a freshman she was named the school's outstanding actress, an unprecedented honor for a first-year student. Playing a wide variety of

roles, she retained her title throughout her college years. Then she moved on to San Diego's famed Globe Theatre.

After being honored with San Diego's annual newspaper award as the city's best actress, she moved over to La Jolla's summer theatre and was encouraged by director Mel Ferrer to try Hollywood.

Signed by Paramount Pictures, where she has now returned for "Happy Days," she made her screen debut as Patricia Crowley's roommate in *Forever Female*.

After appearing in *The Glenn Miller Story*, she again was called by Paramount for increasingly important roles in *Legend of the Incas, Sabrina,* and *The Proud and the Profane*.

Her first major television break came as the winsome Irish maid in "Life With Father," during three years with the CBS-TV series. Later she co-starred with Keith Andes in "Paradise Bay," an NBC-TV daytime series.

The prestigious Margaret Sullavan role in the "Dinner at Eight" TV special added to her acclaim. She has been one of the medium's busiest performers ever since.

Just prior to beginning "Happy Days," she returned to San Diego's Globe Theatre to win outstanding critical notices in Tennessee Williams' *Summer and Smoke,* starring as Alma Winemeiller.

Divorced, Marion lives in Tarzana, California with her two children, Jim, born in 1960, and Ellen, born in 1963.

Because she lived through the Fifties, playing the role of a Fifties mother and being a mother in real life has provided Marion with a unique perspective on the changing status of women in the last twenty years.

"Women in the Fifties were not exposed to life as they are now, but they usually got their way at home," she says. "They were quiet, yet their presence was felt in a totally different way.

"Women of today have gone way out to prove the feminist viewpoint and demand equal rights. Now I think many of them would be just as happy to go back to the more traditional values of wife and mother."

VITAL STATISTICS

Birthdate: October 25
Birthplace: Albert Lea, Minn.
Height: 5'5"
Weight: 120 lbs.
Hair: Brunette
Eyes: Green

ERIN MORAN
(Joanie Cunningham)

© by Paramount Pictures Corporation

Erin Moran

Erin Moran, another member of the "Happy Days" cast who's no newcomer to show business, has been acting since she was six years old.

Actually, "Happy Days" is Erin's second series. She co-starred earlier as Jenny in the "Daktari" series, and, of course, has also guested in numerous other shows.

Erin is the youngest daughter among the six children of Sharon and Edward Moran. Her father is a finance manager and her younger brother John appears in TV commercials.

Erin, tutored at the studio while working

in "Happy Days," has completed studies at Walter Reed Junior High School and is now a student at North Hollywood High.

Blue-eyed, brown-haired Erin was born October 18 in Burbank, California. After a number of TV commercials, she won her first role in a pilot, "Stanley vs. the System," which didn't sell. Her first feature film was *How Sweet It Is*, starring Debbie Reynolds, and this was followed by "Daktari."

Besides guesting in such series as "The Courtship of Eddie's Father" and "Gunsmoke," Erin portrayed Don Rickles' daughter in thirteen episodes of "The Don Rickles Show."

Erin has also appeared with Wayne Newton in the movie *80 Steps to Jonah* and with Godfrey Cambridge in *Watermelon Man*.

Since landing her role in "Happy Days," Erin has made appearances on "The Dinah Shore Show" and in "The Waltons."

VITAL STATISTICS

Birthday: October 18
Birthplace: Burbank, Calif.
Height: 5'3"
Weight: 105 lbs.
Hair: Brown
Eyes: Blue

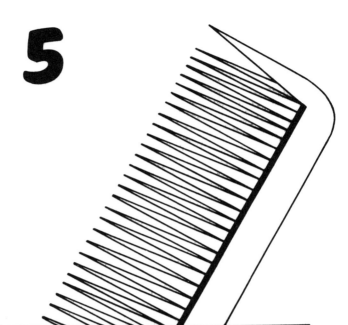

5

The Making of "Happy Days"

The Making of "Happy Days"

To most of us outsiders, producing a television comedy seems more like play than work. Nothing could be further from the truth. Writing, staging, and filming a weekly series, not to mention all the business aspects of the process, involves the talent and intensive efforts of a slew of individuals, of which the actors are only one part. From story concept to filmic representation, hard work—very hard work—is the operative principle.

For many of those involved it is a labor of love, but labor nonetheless.

And it begins with an idea—a kernel of the situation that eventually will become a complete story, interesting, perhaps heart-warming, and, of course, humorous. In the case of "Happy Days," this kernel may be spawned by producer Garry Marshall, any of the five-man writing staff headed by Bob Brunner, an outside freelance writer, or even a fan.

Occasionally a freelance writer will actually create the entire script. If not, the story seed is developed by the writing staff. But this is only the beginning of a long, arduous task. The rest is best described by director/producer Jerry Paris, beginning with his notions of the director's role in bringing the script to fruition.

Director/Producer Jerry Paris Talks About the Making of the Show

Primarily, a director's job is to direct actors, not cameras. When most people visit a studio they only hear the director say, "Action," and "Cut and print it." They think that's all he does, but it all starts with the director working on the script—if he's a good director—even before the actors enter the picture.

I serve as a director/producer on the "Happy Days" series. The first year I was only directing. I didn't write the scripts, but I'd get them before the actors saw them and I'd make notes on my suggested changes. Then we'd read it over at a table and I'd pitch in as much as the writers and the producers. Garry Marshall recognized that I might not have the answer to a scene as a writer would, but I know when it works and when it won't comedically. That's something I learned through men like Carl Reiner, who I worked with for five years doing "The Dick Van Dyke Show."

Then when you get to the stage, you know how a scene should be played and you can start directing the actors. And as you direct, you invent. You have to move the actor in a direction so that he or she understands the script and can transfer the author's intent on paper onto the stage. In this sense, the director is like the conductor of a symphony orchestra who says, "No, that's too much French horn."

But of course most of the time the composer is long dead and conflicts don't arise. With the script writers watching your every move, conflicts are inevitable. I win some points and I lose some. But that's part of the process.

Now this will give some idea of what one week is like getting a "Happy Days" episode together.

On Monday morning at ten o'clock, the actors come in, sit around a table and for the first time see the script for the following week's show. We read it through

Then we go to the current script which we've read the week before and changed according to the last week's meeting. Now the actors read it. Maybe they're a little

A quick bite between scenes.
© by Paramount Pictures Corporation

Henry double-checks a line during a rehearsal.
© by Paramount Pictures Corporation

thoroughly and play it to the best of our ability even if the actors aren't quite sure of the intent. The writers are there and they're making notes. I'm taking notes and Garry's taking notes—"Not funny," "This doesn't work here," "Bad line for Fonzie." Now the actors are questioned about their feelings of the script.

We'll then have a short meeting about this "pink script," record our notes, and then the writers will take it back, having a rough idea of where to start making changes.

Henry and Ron take five during rehearsal of "The Not Making of a President" episode.
© by Paramount Pictures Corporation

disappointed, maybe they thought it would be better. We take notes and then the actors go to lunch.

For the next couple of hours, the writers and I stay and punch up the script. When the actors get back, if there's room on the set (if it's not under construction), I'll take them in and work for about two hours with the scenes that are in good shape. In the meantime, the writers are working out the scenes that need changing.

On Tuesday, there'll be a few changes, a few "blue pages" added, and now I'm on my own until Wednesday at three when we'll do a run-through of the show with my changes, giving the best performance possible without costumes and without carrying the scripts because the actors have already learned their lines. In the few days that I've worked with them I try new things. I'm not tied down to the script. If things didn't work, I may have gone another way. I may have restaged something or changed or added jokes.

Also on Wednesday, the actors again have an opportunity to say what they feel about the revised script. When they leave in the evening, Garry, the writers, and myself go upstairs to the conference room, we order terrible food that we get from a terrible restaurant, and we start to write. And we write until about eleven o'clock in the night. We change, we rewrite, and we rework. We call it "futzing"—take the good things from Jerry, take the good things from the writers, etc. We pitch and sometimes it takes an hour to get one little moment. Then we turn that script into a "yellow script" for all the cameramen because on Thursday morning, we do camera blocking.

So Thursday we block the show. At ten a.m. the actors have the revised script and we walk it through and the stand-ins come

Ron looks over some production notes—there are plenty of them. © by Paramount Pictures Corporation

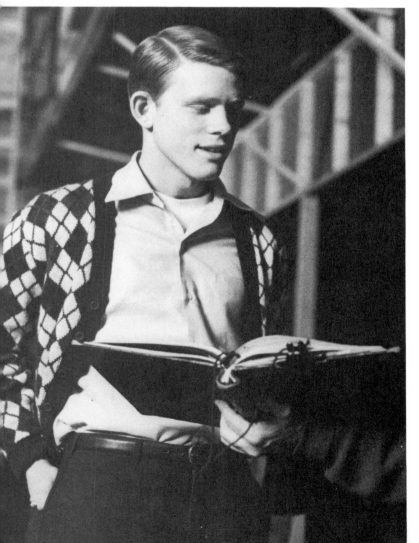

in while I block the cameras and the actors practice their lines with my assistant dialogue man, my right arm—Bob Hoffman, who runs the scene backstage with them. He's been with me ever since my first movie, *Never a Dull Moment*, with Edward G. Robinson.

We use a theater stage technique for filming, with three 35mm motion picture cameras on crab dollies. In most television, there's only one cameraman zooming and focusing on everything. We have to have one man operating the camera, one on the side focusing because we do zooming, and one guy pushing the camera on the dolly. Those three men follow the actors with the cameras. The center camera is what we call "the master shot," which is the shot of three or four people in the scene. The side cameras are the "close up" or "cross angle tight" shots, singles or over the shoulder. It's very important that every camera has a position for every shot. If we were doing a one-camera show it would take three days to film a half-hour comedy that we now do in one day.

When I'm through blocking the cameras, around five or six o'clock, we have another run-through and the writers sit up in the stands and we're all making more notes. Then after the crew leaves, the actors give their impressions and they go home.

Then it's back up to the conference room until eleven o'clock with the terrible food and we do the final polish. We add a few "gold pages" to the yellow script and the camera coordinator, the man who calls the shots from the booth, also has to note the changes because sometimes we've changed or dropped or added a line. He's got to know every change so the cameramen can follow the action. Sometimes, for example, with the filming of the "Fonzie Loves Pinky" episodes, a whole scene has to be restaged because of such unforeseen things as not being able to get the shot you wanted because the hood of a car is lifted and blocking the camera.

You see, our show is shot like other shows, such as "All in the Family" or "Rhoda" or "The Mary Tyler Moore Show," except that in these shows, which are all marvelous, there may only be two or three people in a scene ninety percent of the time. But in "Happy Days" we have twenty-five extras every week, dancing, eating at the drive-in, we have music cues, we have six or seven people in the Cunninghams' living room. It's really a one-camera exterior show but we've made it a three-camera show because the humor demands it.

Now it's Friday and we run through each scene twice without an audience, starting at noon, with the changes from Thursday night. Now is when we really work on performance.

At four we do another run-through before an audience and then we all get together in the living room set with the network people and right up to the last minute we're making changes. The actors grab a bite to eat and go into make-up. I put on my lucky red sweater and we're ready for the filming. Garry comes out and introduces the cast, then I'm introduced, and I in turn introduce my crew, my assistant, dialogue coach, and script girl. We bring the actors out and I tell my assistant to "Roll 'em." The cameras roll and I say, "Action."

During the course of the filming, the actors may make mistakes. If they make a

Henry grimaces in the background while Ron and Anson relax beside the cars used in the drag race episode. © by Paramount Pictures Corporation

verbal mistake I'll back them up while we're rolling. Or, after the scene's over, we'll grab a few of what we call "pickups"—a quick shot of Fonzie, a better exit because the cameraman made a mistake and opened the lens when he should have closed down on it or vice versa. If we start to lose the audience because of too many re-takes, we'll just write down the mistakes and do it when we're done filming at about nine-fifteen to about ten-thirty.

If we do, though, we'll use the original laugh track. We won't put one on. It's not fair. Carl Reiner used to say, "If you don't get a laugh it wasn't funny and doesn't deserve a laugh."

Then when it's all over we collapse and go our separate ways for the weekend.

We'll do ten shows in a row like that with a week's break in September, come back and do twelve shows in a row until Christmas, and if we're picked up, we work January and then go our own ways until June.

I think Carl Reiner summed up the process we go through perfectly when he said, "On Monday you pick up the bobsled and you start going to the top of the hill. And you're not ready to slide down that hill until you film on Friday at about eight p.m. and the director says action. Then it's back up the hill Monday morning."

Coming into the home stretch, Ron, Anson, Henry, and Tom break on the set of the Cunninghams' living room. © by Paramount Pictures Corporation

6

"And...Action!"

"And . . . Action!"

The Paramount lot is dreamland. Fantasies are born here in this sprawling motion picture factory tucked away on a parcel of land bordered by Gower Street, Van Ness, and Melrose Avenues in Hollywood. It is a distinctive land—immediately impressive to the outsider and marked by the paradoxical air of Hollywood glamour and the anxious, technical business of producing entertainment.

The atmosphere is awesome and powerful, quite like Washington, D.C. For here, at one of the oldest studios in Hol-

Behind these gates fantasies are born. "Happy Days" is one of them.
© by Paramount Pictures Corporation

lywood, lurk the specters of stars and motion pictures gone, though engraved in the history of an industry that is peculiarly American. And here are made the decisions that may ultimately end in reels of celluloid film, distributed perhaps throughout the world, sparking laughter and tears, touching the inner and often very personal nerves of audiences, formulating values and quite possibly the aspirations that drive the American people.

And the fantasies die here too. Sets are torn down, make-up is washed away, scripts are filed, and costumes are stored for future dreams. All that is left are the images on film and the memories in people's minds. The stars, the writers, the directors, the behind-the-scenes personnel—all walk away and become just regular people, moving on to another film, another episode.

On the way from the DeMille building to Sound Stage 19, home of "Happy Days," dream remnants abound—a few fake street scenes (one of 19th-century Western American vintage, the other a row of porno bookstores and movie houses) and, piled up in a crowded storage area, a huge blue-sky backdrop, an artificial gray mountain, and other bygone props. Except for these giveaways, the alleys that run behind the buildings might be walkways at a rubber band factory. The contrast is distracting.

So, too, the large, barnlike structure ahead seen from its rear could be anything . . . except for the simple, unglamorous sign above it, "Stage 19."

Then through the rickety door, past the undistinguishable wires and parapher-

W. A. **0436**
Series: **HAPPY DAYS**
Producer: **TONY MARSHALL/PARIS**
Director: **JERRY PARIS**
Title: **"FONZIE LOVES PINKY PT I"**
3-PARTER INTERIORS

CALL SHEET
Prod. No **60534-722**

Day **FRIDAY, JULY 23, 1976**
5th Day out of **5** days
CREW Call **12N**
CAST Call **1230P**
Location **STAGE 19**

SET # SET	SCENES	CAST	D/N	PAGES	LOCATION
	CAST REHEARSAL				STAGE 19
	RUN-THRU @ 4 P.M.				EXT. 1919
	SHOOT SHOW @ 750 P.M.				
	CLOSED SET UNTIL RUN-THRU @ 4P				

CAST & DAY PLAYERS	PART OF	MAKE-UP/LEAVE	SET CALL	REMARKS
RON HOWARD	RICHIE		1230P	
HENRY WINKLER	FONZIE			
ANSON WILLIAMS	POTSIE			
MARION ROSS	MARION			
TOM BOSLEY	HOWARD			
DONNY MOST	RALPH			
ERIN MORAN #	JOANIE		130P	
AL MOLINARO	AL		1230P	
ROZ KELLY	PINKY			
DORIS HESS	TINA			
KELLY SANDERS	LOLA			
MICHAEL PATAKI	COUNT MALLACHI			
KEN LERNER	ROCCO MALLACHI			
BETH CLOPTON - TEACHER @ 130P				
# MINOR				

ATMOSPHERE AND STANDINS	SPECIAL INSTRUCTIONS
B STAND-INS @ 1230P	
ATMOS. W/N	

ADVANCE SHOOTING NOTES

SHOOTING DATE	SET NO.	SET NAME	LOCATION	SCENE NO.
MON., 7/26/76		CAST READING #722 "FONZIE LOVES PINKY, PT II" (3-PARTER INTERIORS)	GOWER REHEARSAL HALL	EXT. 1388
TUES, 7/27/76		CAST BLOCKING	STAGE 19	EXT. 1919
WED, 7/28/76		CAST REHEARSAL & BLOCKING		
THURS, 7/29/76		CAST REHEARSAL & CAMERA BLOCKING		

UNIT PROD. MGR. **JOHN THOMAS LENOX** PHONE **2214** ASST. DIR **R.J. STONE/N. PELLEGRINO** PHONE **1919**
ART DIR. **MONTY ELLIOTT** PHONE **2578** SET DEC. **ANDY NEALIS** PHONE **1180**
ISSUED BY OPERATIONS: DATE **7-22-76** TIME **810P** APPROVED

MD 300-1

—the call sheets for any given day's work are pretty self-explanatory. Essentially, they are detailed time

HAPPY DAYS   60534
PRODUCTION : "FONZIE LOVES PINKY, PT. I"   722   DATE FRI, 7/23 ,1976 W. A **0436**
3- PARTER INTERIORS

	NO.	ITEM	TIME	CHARGE	REMARKS		NO.	ITEM	TIME	CHARGE	REMARKS
PRODUCTION		EXTRA ASST DIRECTOR	—	705-04		MAKE-UP	1	MAKE-UP MAN	1P	760-01	
	1	2ND ASST DIRECTOR	—	705-04			1	EXTRA MAKE UP MAN	1 30p	760-02	
	1	CAMERA COORD	12N				1	BODY MAKE UP WOMAN	W/N	760-03	
	1	SCRIPT SUPERVISOR	12N	705-06			1	HAIR STYLIST	1P	760-04	
							1	EXTRA HAIR STYLISTS	1 30p	760-05	
		DIALOGUE COACH		620-05							
CAMERA	1	CAMERAMAN	12N	710-01		ELECTRICAL	1	GAFFER	12N	730-01	
	3	OPERATOR	12 18P	710-02			1	BEST BOY	12N	730-01	
	3	ASSISTANT	12 12P	710-03			4	LAMP OPERATOR	12N	730-02	
	1	ASSISTANT	3P	710-04	STICK MAN		2	MOTORCYCLE BATTERIES	12N		
	3	BNCR CAMERAS	12 12P	710-08	6 TO 1 ZOOMS			WIND MACHINE & OPERATOR		725-22	
		EXTRA OPERATOR		710-02			X	GENERATOR & OPERA.	1 36A	730	POWER TO 19
		EXTRA ASSISTANT		710-04			X	AIR COND. & HEAT	W/N	725-22	STAGE 19
				710/920				OPERATIONS PHONE		725-21	
SET OPERATIONS	1	KEY GRIP	12N	725-01			X	PORTABLE TELEPHONE	11 30A	725-21	
	1	2ND GRIP	12N	725-01			X	WIG WAG		725-21	
		EXTRA GRIPS		725-02			X	WORK LIGHTS	↙	725-21	STAGE 19 & 20
		CRANE OPERATOR		725-03		POLICE & FIRE	1	FIREMAN	3 45P	725/775	
	3	CRAB DOLLY GRIP	12 12P	725-03				FIRE WARDEN LOC.		775	
	3	CRAB DOLLY	12 12P	725-05				WHISTLEMEN		725	
		BOOM #		725-06			1	WATCHMAN	12 30P	725/775	
	1	CRAFT SERVICE MAN	12N	725-11							
		GREENSMAN		725-13				CITY POLICE		775-02	
	1	PAINTER	12N	725-14			1	STUDIO POLICE	3 30P	725-15	WINDSOR GATE
		PLUMBER		725-17				MOTORCYCLE POLICE		775-02	
		PROP MAKERS		735-04			1	FIRST AID	3 45P	725/775	
		SPEC. EFFECTS MEN		735-01-02		MISCELLANEOUS		PROCESS EQUIPMENT		780	
		WIND MACH.		735-08				PROCESS CAMERAMAN		780-02	
		WARD CHECK ROOM		725-23				PROCESS ASST. CAMERAMAN		780-02	
		BENCHES FOR PEOPLE		725-25				PROCESS GRIPS		780-04	
		KNOCK DOWN SCH. ROOMS		725-23				PROCESS ELECT.		780-04	
		KNOCK DOWN DR ROOMS		725-23				PROJECTION MACHINE		780-08	
	8	PORTABLE DR. ROOMS	12N	725-23	AS IS STG. 19			PROJECTIONIST PROCESS		780-03	
		HOOK-UP DR. ROOMS		725-21	ALL ROOMS CLEAN			FILM		785-01	
		SCHOOLROOM TRAILERS		725-24	LIT & READY						
	5	DRESSING RMS TRAILERS	12N	725-24	BY 12 N	MUSIC		PIANO		810-6	
		OUTSIDE 19						SIDELINE ORCHESTRA		810-6	
SOUND	1	SOUND MIXER	12N	765-01				SINGERS		810-6	
	2	MIKE MAN	12N	765-02		CATERER		HOT LUNCHES		775/790	
	1	SOUND RECORDER	2 30P	765-03				BOX LUNCHES		775/790	
	1	CABLE MAN	12N	765-04	UTILITY		105	DINNERS	5 30P	775/790	STAGE 21
		EXTRA CABLE MAN		765-04			5	GALLONS OF COFFEE	12N	775/790	OBLATH'S: DELIVER
		P. A. SYSTEM		765-06				GALLONS		775/790	TO STAGE 19
		PLAYBACK MACH. & OP.		765-07-05				DOZEN DOUGHNUTS		775/790	
		SOUND SYSTEM		765		TRANSPORTATION	1	STANDBY DRIVER	3P	770/775	STAGE 19
PROPERTY	1	PROPERTY MAN	11 36A	750-01			1	STANDBY CAR	3P	770/775	↙
	1	ASST. PROPERTY MAN	11 36A	750-01				CAMERA TRUCK		770/775	
		EXTRA ASST. PROP. MAN		750-02				ELECTRIC TRUCK		770/775	
	1	SET DRESSER	W/N	745-01	SPLIT		X	CAMERA PU	12 12P		LOT TRACTOR
	1	LEAD MAN	W/N	745-02				GENERATOR TRUCK		770/775	
		DRAPERY MAN		725-18				GRIP TRUCK		770/775	
	1	SWING GANG MAN	W/N	745-02	SPLIT			PROP. TRUCK		770/775	
		WARDROBE RACKS		725-25				SPEC. EFFECTS TRUCK		770/775	
		MAKE-UP TABLES		725-25				SET DRESSING TRUCK		770/775	
		HAIR DRESSING TABLES		725-25				WARDROBE TRUCK/ TRAILER		770/775	
		ANIMALS		750-06				WATER WAGON		770/775	
								SANITARY UNIT		775	
		HANDLERS		750-07				TRUCKS		770/775	
		A. H. A. MAN		750-07							
		WRANGLERS		750-07							
		WAGONS. ETC.		750-08				BUSSES		770/775	
WARDROBE	1	COSTUMER MEN	12N	755-01				PICTURE CARS		750-05	
	1	COSTUMER WOMEN	12N	755-02			2	MOTORCYCLES	12N		
		EXTRA COST. MEN		755-03			3	CARS	12N		
		EXTRA COST. WOMEN		755-03							

MISC. NOTES **SECURITY: PLEASE LEAVE LEMON GROVE GATE OPEN UNTIL 12 MID.**

nalia . . . and bang! Familiarity. Almost. Stretching lengthwise across the studio is the "Happy Days" set—but not just the Cunninghams' living room, or Arnold's. No, they are all there, including Bronko's Repair Shop. The fantasy would be obvious were there only one set. But strung end-to-end, the right wall of one room serving also as the left wall of the one adjacent, it is glaring.

And the people milling around—stagehands, writers, cameramen—they could be anyone off the street in the 1970s. But they are parading around, doing their jobs, hustling and bustling among the tables and juke box in Arnold's and the furniture in the Cunninghams' 1950s living room. Again, the contrast is remarkable.

It's July 23. A Friday. "Happy Days" is in its final stages before the interior filming of "Fonzie Loves Pinky," Part I. During the week, the script has been re-worked, the parts rehearsed and the camera instructions developed. Now, at about 4:30 in the afternoon, the cast and crew are ready to undertake the run-through, an exact replica (down to the blocking of cameras) of what will be filmed in three hours.

As the stagehands put the final touches on the sets, hammers banging, a few of the actors drift out on the set. Henry Winkler glances blankly at the group assembled to watch the run-through. Dressed in a checked shirt, jeans, and a pair of boots, he seems miles away from Fonzie. All along he has insisted that he and his "Happy Days" counterpart are distinctly different individuals. That now appears very clear as the slight-framed actor, hair stylishly cut in a way that seems the exact opposite of Fonzie's greased-back DA, shuffles back behind the stage.

Tom Bosley is a walking paradox. The head is Howard Cunningham's (except the eyeglasses resting on the end of his nose). The rest, however, is obviously Tom

Henry dons a helmet in preparation for the filming of a demolition derby scene, shot a week prior to the interior filming of the same episode.
© by Paramount Pictures Corporation

Bosley—loose white shirt, casually fitting French-cut jeans, and a pair of loafers.

Only Ron Howard is unstartling. A larger version of Opie Taylor, he looks like a young boy just back from a sandlot baseball game. On anyone else, the striped polo shirt, baggy blue jeans, and tennis shoes might look slightly comical. Of those who grew up with his childhood role on "The Andy Griffith Show," though, who has ever imagined Ron Howard any differently?

The temperature rises in the studio, no doubt due in part to the thousands of watts of light glaring down on the set. A few more people file in to watch the proceedings. Among them is Dom DeLuise and family. Also, across the way, is Lee Merriwether of "Barnaby Jones." The preponderance of stars at arm's length increases the excitement. For those on stage, it's just another day's work. For those in the audience it's really nothing new. But for the non-show-biz folk it's a revealing, maybe thrilling, peek at what goes on before the television does.

Amid the giggling, chattering, and on-stage preparations, director/producer Jerry Paris looks calm (maybe it's just fatigue). Quite frankly, he radiates competence. Like Ron Howard, this television veteran holds a certain spot in the hearts of those who grew up in the 1960s. As Rob Petrie's next-door neighbor on "The Dick Van Dyke Show," Jerry Paris presented a humorous, lighthearted, and dependable nature that seems, after all these years, to be his own.

Finally all is ready for the run-through. All attention is focused to the far right of the stage, the Cunninghams' living room.

The cameras jockey into position. Quiet.

"And action," yells Paris.

Into the room bursts Howard, sporting a bizarre leopard-print fez. Suddenly, the cameras and all extraneous personnel and equipment fade out of the picture. It is "Happy Days" and "Happy Days" alone. Only it's live "Happy Days."

Howard tells Marion about the flyers he, as chairman of the Leopard's Lodge demolition derby, has prepared. It's funny, it's polished (in fact flawless), and there's no television screen between us and the Cunninghams—nothing to render them all merely two-dimensional pictures that will be interrupted by commercials.

"And dissolve out," Paris signals the end of the scene.

The scurrying begins again, as stagehands push two Fifties-model cars into Bronko's Repair Shop (one of which is

Fonzie communicates with his partner Pinky Tuscadero, who's driving another car in the demolition derby.

by Paramount Pictures Corporation

the Cunninghams' DeSoto). But such work is not the sole responsibility of the hands, evidenced by producer Garry Marshall toting a drum set over to the side of the stage—a rather unexpected sight. But, as Paris explains, "He's the only one here who knows how to set them up."

The left wall of Arnold's is swung into the malt shop, thus widening Bronko's, and the action begins as Richie enters to talk to Fonzie about his role as commentator on the upcoming demolition derby.

"Okay, reset," says Paris, notifying the cameramen to change their angles. A few props are moved, the cameras shift in a strange mechanical waltz and Ralph struts in begging Fonzie to let him drive in the demolition derby.

"Ralph, people get hurt," Fonzie warns him, as the boom mike hovers above and follows them around the stage like a circling hawk.

"That's okay," Ralph replies with unfounded bravado. "I can take it."

"Ralph, people get maimed," Fonzie says coolly, anticipating Ralph's response.

"Maimed?" Ralph gulps. And suddenly he remembers he's got a stiff neck and maybe he shouldn't get involved.

But the real revelation is that Fonzie has pulled the radiator from Howard's car to use in his own demolition car. He and Richie have all they can do to calm Howard when he discovers what's happened.

But Howard's main concern is that he has nothing to drive to the demolition derby.

"Now Mr. C., would I leave you without trans?" Fonzie asks as he escorts Howard to a small motor scooter.

The boys finally get him to sit down on the scooter. Fonzie steps back as if examining a fine piece of artwork.

"Mr. C., you look like Brando in *The Wild One*," he observes.

A smile breaks across Paris' face. What memories this must spur for him, for somewhere in the crowd of black leather jackets in that 1952 film was Paris himself, a young aspiring actor.

Meanwhile, as the scene winds down, Garry Marshall, periodically glancing at the action on the adjacent set, madly scribbles notes at a table in Arnold's.

Both of these little off-stage vignettes remind us that behind the "Happy Days" we see on Tuesday nights are real people, working long and hard to make us laugh.

"And dissolve."

The crew jumps back to action, pushing back the wall shared by Bronko's and Arnold's (how tiny Arnold's is in real life) and putting salt and pepper shakers, partially consumed pizzas, and Cokes on the tables. The Arnold's crowd begins to drift in—a melange of saddle-shoed Fifties characters—and in the background, peering out of the window between the kitchen and the malt shop, is the basset-hound face of Al (played by Al Molinaro), the new proprietor of Arnold's (Arnold having moved on to another fantasy). On the back wall of Arnold's is a sign reading "Milwaukee Team Demolition Derby."

The following three photos give some indication of the incongruity of a run-through. Notice the hair and clothing styles—definitely not Fifties. In the second and third shots, Henry further confuses the image by donning Fonzie's leather jacket over his street clothes. The scene is from "Fonzie the Superstar," shown in Chapter Three in its polished form.
© by Paramount Pictures Corporation

Ron Howard and Anson Williams linger off to the left where the off-stage band is taking up some time playing a lively jazz tune.

Paris' voice from somewhere, "And we dissolve to the sign."

After Richie and Potsie play a rendition of "You're Sixteen," Al is called upon to make a welcoming speech. He balks, but finally the portly, comical figure takes the stage. Barely a sentence leaves his mouth and Dom Deluise erupts into laughter. It's funny, possibly funnier than the filmed version—one of life's little mysteries.

Eventually we meet Pinky Tuscadero, a . . . well, let's say well-proportioned young lady who is in many ways a Fonzie spin-off in pink hot pants. We find out that Fonzie's partner in the demolition derby can't make it. We see Ralph, the nightmare of himself maimed still fresh in his mind, ready to run for the hills when Fonzie appoints him to replace his partner. And we see Pinky, red with anger (to mix a

metaphor) that Fonzie won't let her race with him.

Finally, in the second to last scene, Fonzie, enraged by Pinky's having taken up with his arch demolition derby rival, Count Mallachi, decides that Pinky can, alas, drive with him. His announcement comes after a swift blow to the juke box silences the music in Arnold's, alerting the crowd to his presence.

But as Pinky and Fonzie sip Cokes lovingly in Arnold's, all is not well at Bronko's as the fiend, Count Mallachi, brings a sledgehammer down on Pinky's pink Chevrolet on the adjacent set.

"And dissolve out."

Outside, the line to see the "Happy Days" filming wraps around from Melrose Avenue part way up Gower. It doesn't seem possible they'll all get into Stage 19. Too bad. But perhaps those who won't will in some way be better off. For them the fantasy will remain intact.

7

Fonzie's
"Foto Album"

"At ease." Henry, Ron, and Tom pause during the "Fonzie Loves Pinky" run-through to mull over some last minute changes. Photo by Norm Robbins

The gang tries to cheer the ailing Fonzie as he lies in his hospital bed. © by Paramount Pictures Corporation

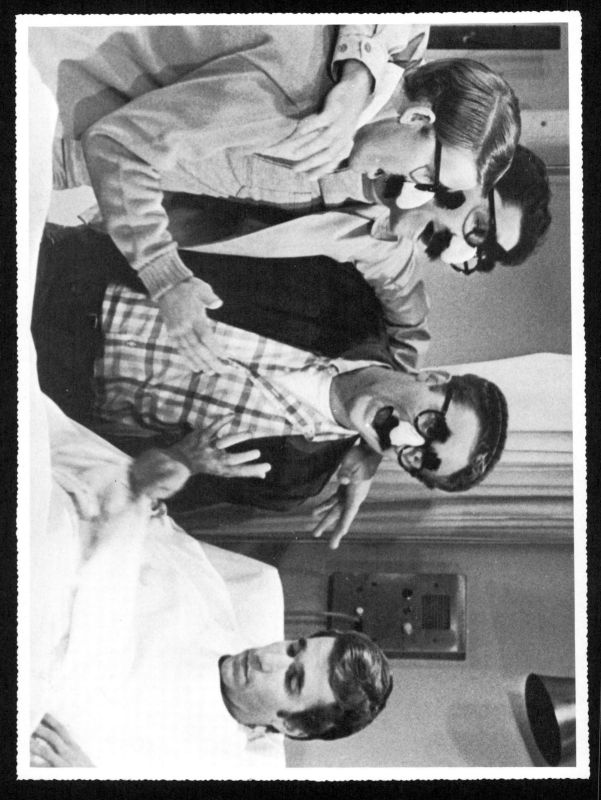

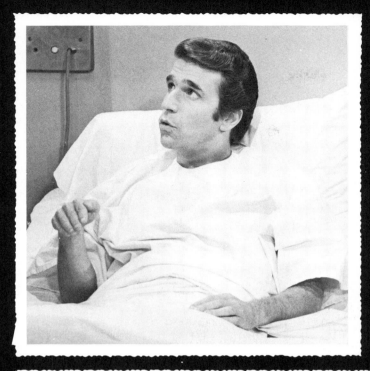

"Your knee looks fine . . . mine don't move." © by Paramount Pictures Corporation

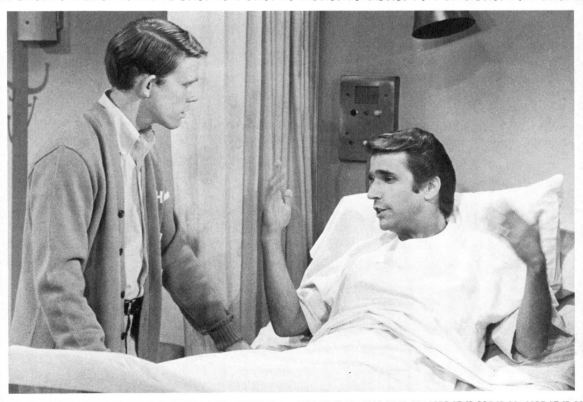

The Fonz lays out the problem.
© by Paramount Pictures Corporation

Howard to Fonzie: "You certainly have a healthy attitude." © by Paramount Pictures Corporation

The Cunninghams decide to tell Fonzie his motorcycle is on fire in the hope he'll get on his feet and walk. © by Paramount Pictures Corporation

The Fonz is reluctant to stop acting sick. If his motorcycle is on fire, why don't the Cunninghams put it out? © by Paramount Pictures Corporation

Fonzie insists he is not putting his injured foot on the floor until he can do it "cool." © by Paramount Pictures Corporation

The Fonz says he can't talk to people who want him to be uncool.
© by Paramount Pictures Corporation

"Fearless Fonzarelli's record-breaking leap" is replayed for an enthusiastic audience. © by Paramount Pictures Corporation

Of course the leg hurts, Fonzie tells Richie. Why else would he be going "ooh, ooh?"
© by Paramount Pictures Corporation

"Play ball!" All photos in the softball sequence by Ben Davidson.

He may not be Tom Seaver, but he's sure got style!

The wind up. . . .

And the pitch.

Donny Most shows his winning style at the plate.

This one may be headed for the center field bleachers.